COLORS @ mnp

Written by **Kristin Gies** & **Peter Tonn** • Illustrated by **Hannah Tews**

MEQUON *Nature Preserve*

The insects at MNP can be found in many shapes, sizes, and colors.

BLACK

Explore the trails to see
which ones you can find.
MNP trails are open to the
public every day of the year,
from sunrise to sunset,
at no charge.

Sowbugs

Boxelder Bug

Giant Water Bug

Carpenter Ant

Green

YELLOW

Four-Lined Plant Bug

Regal Moth

Assassin Bug

Monarch Butterfly

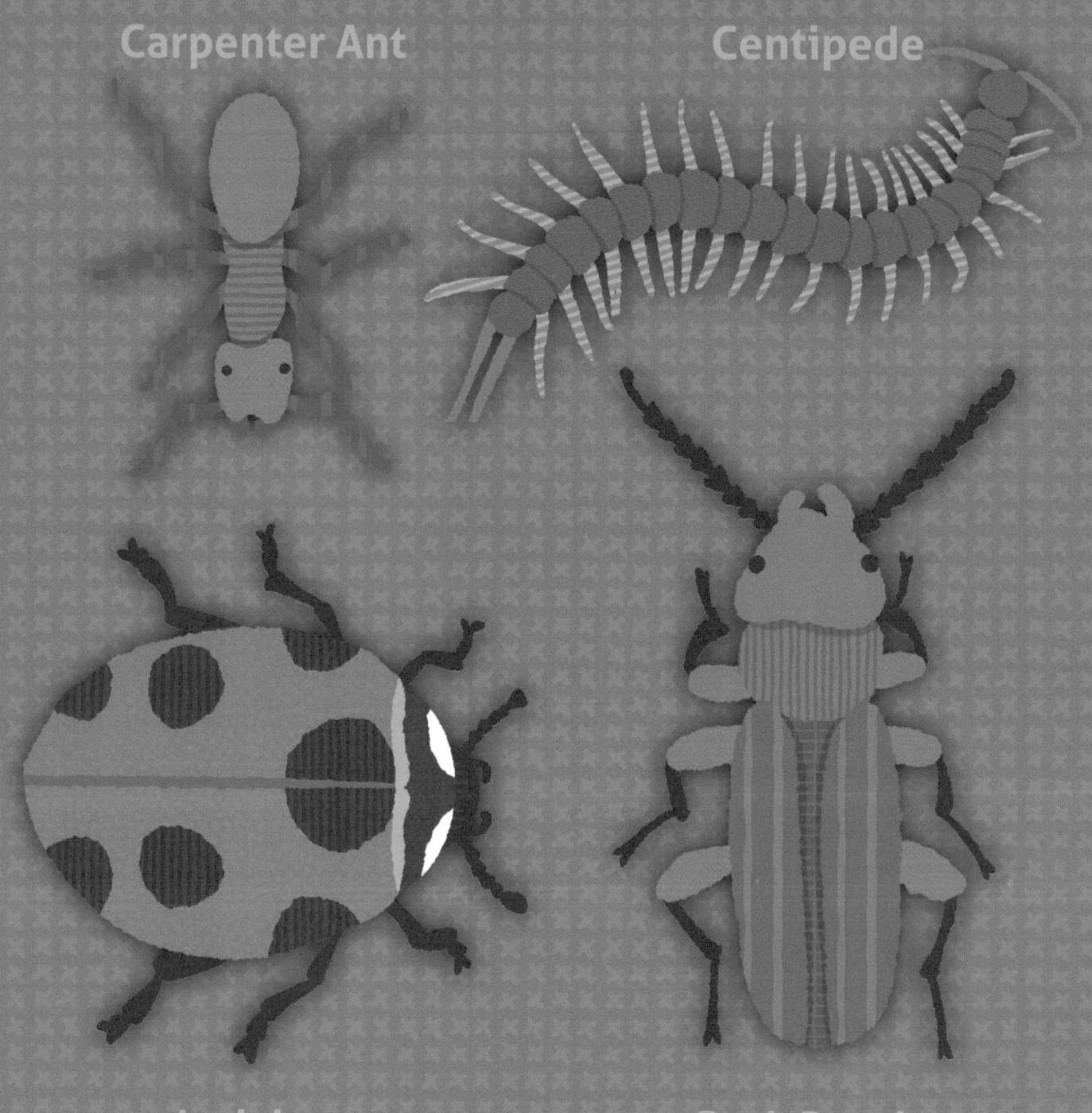

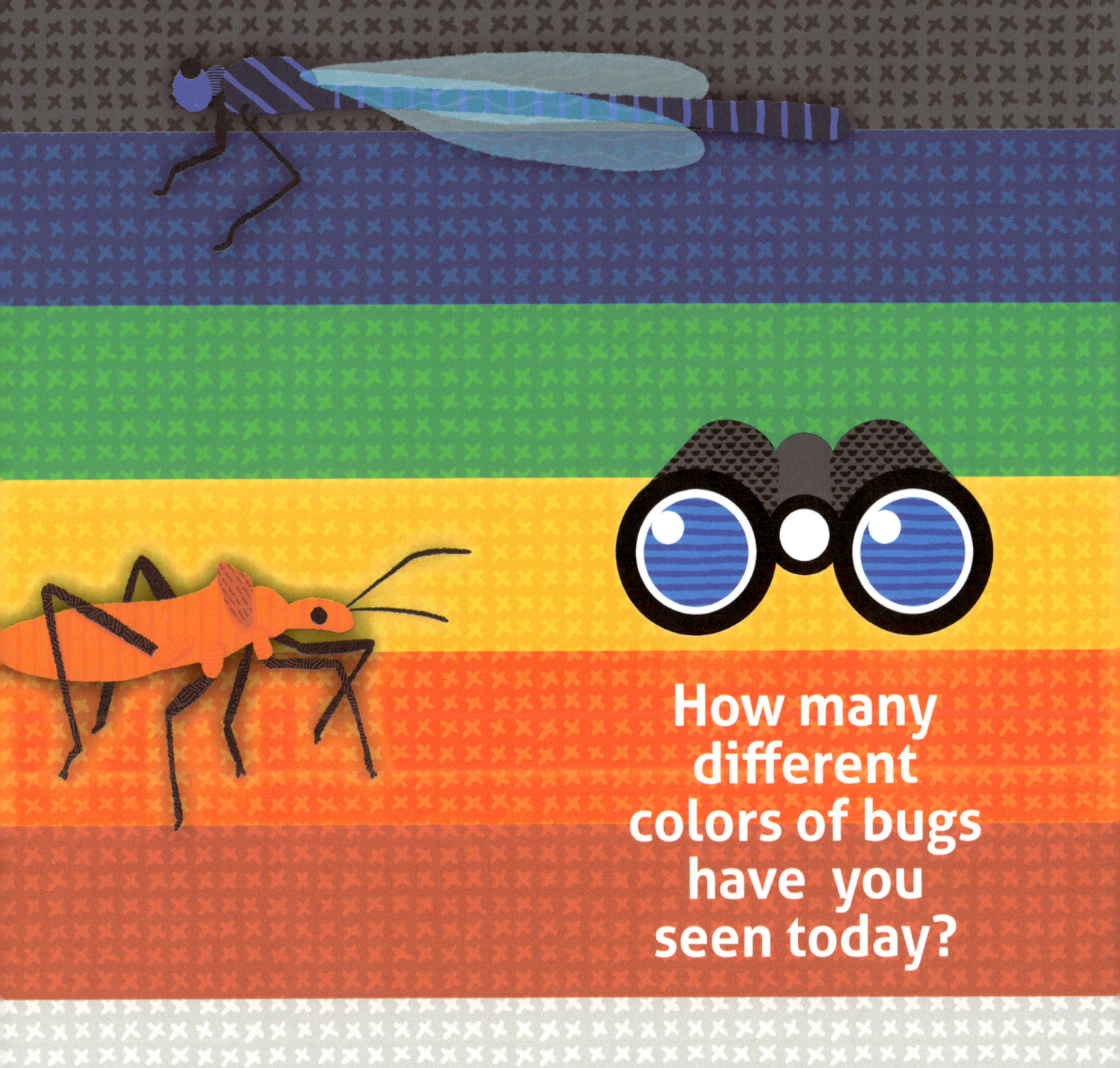

How many different colors of bugs have you seen today?

Mequon Nature Preserve is a 510-acre active land restoration site and living laboratory where you can explore, discover, breathe, learn, and help restore 5 different ecosystems. There are no trail fees, no membership fees, just come enjoy, reconnect with the land, and watch the transformation happen right before your eyes. Just 20 years into a 150-year restoration plan, 80,000 trees and shrubs have been planted. Thirty acres of wetland restored and hundreds of native wildlife and plant species are now thriving thanks to donors, community partners, and volunteers who all come together in concert to make this incredible transformation possible.

MEQUON *Nature Preserve*

Published by Orange Hat Publishing 2023
HC ISBN: 9781645387596

Copyrighted © 2023 by Kristin Gies and Peter Tonn
All Rights Reserved
Colors@MNP
Written by Kristin Gies and Peter Tonn
Illustrated by Hannah Tews

This publication and all contents within may not be reproduced or transmitted in any part or in its entirety without the written permission of the author.

orangehatpublishing.com

Printed in the USA
CPSIA information can be obtained
at www.ICGtesting.com
LVHW072133200824
788828LV00012B/48